THE OLYMPICS
Atlanta 1996

Across the curriculum activities

Written by Sandy Sturmer

Published by Prim-Ed Publishing

Foreword

The Olympics, Atlanta 1996 is a set of copymasters designed to maximise interest in the Olympic Games and sport. The copymasters provide the children with primary curriculum activities using the theme, the Olympic Games. Emphasis has been placed on giving the children information about the Olympic Games and sports by using highly motivational activities.

The worksheets are varied, and include language, maths, social studies, health, art and creative writing activities using a thematic approach to this topic.

This book consists of 30 pupil activity worksheets, an individual pupil record sheet and a set of 24 Quiz Questions to conclude the activities. Also included is a cover page which may be used to combine all the worksheets, and perhaps news clippings into a booklet, file or scrapbook to be kept as a record of the Olympics, 1996.

Ideal for use in middle and upper primary areas and also has application for secondary pupils.

Contents

Cover Page ii	Sporting Shapes 17
Early Olympic Games 1	World Records 18
Olympic Symbols 2	Marathon Maths 19
Where are the Games Held? 3	Picture Codes 20
All About Atlanta 4	Team Numbers 21
Medal Tally Sheet 5	Busy as Bees 22
Opening Ceremony - Team Order ... 6	Fit and Healthy Body - 1 23
Read and Draw 7	Fit and Healthy Body - 2 24
Equipment Maze 8	Coins of the USA 25
Measuring Athletes 9	Special People 26
The Olympic Motto 10	Team or Individual Sports? 27
Ideals and Aspirations 11	Disabled Sports 28
Olympic Winner 12	Relaxing is Important 29
Atlanta Road Map 13	Sports Words Jumble 30
Sporting Word Puzzle 14	Children's Record Sheet 31
Good Food for Athletes 15	Quiz Questions 32
Mask of a Greek God 16	Answer Sheet 33

Early Olympic Games

Read the following passage carefully.

It gives you some information about the ancient Olympic Games. Answer the questions which follow the information.

In 776 BC (Before Christ), the first Olympic Games were held. People came to the Temple of Zeus to worship the gods and show their strengths. The prize for the winners of the games was a wild olive wreath.

The Games were held every four years. More events were added as time went by. The athletes lived in luxury and had special coaches. At first, women were not allowed to compete or even see the Games, but in time, women were allowed to watch.

The Olympic Games became a time of peace and friendship. War battles were only fought after the Games were over as it was very important to compete in the Olympic Festival.

1. What was the prize for winning the Games? _____
2. When was the first Olympic Games held? _____
3. True or false?   Women were allowed to compete. _____
4. What two reasons were given for people going to the Temple of Zeus?

    (a) _____

    (b) _____
5. The Olympic Games became a time of _____ and _____.
6. What word tells you the athletes were treated well? _____
7. How often are the Olympic Games held? _____
8. True or false? More types of games were added. _____
9. The Olympic Games were also called the Olympic _____
10. Would you like to have been an athlete? _____ Why? _____

Olympic Symbols

The Olympic Torch and the Olympic Rings are two symbols of the Olympic Games. Read the passages for each, and fill in the spaces using the words on the torch and the rings.

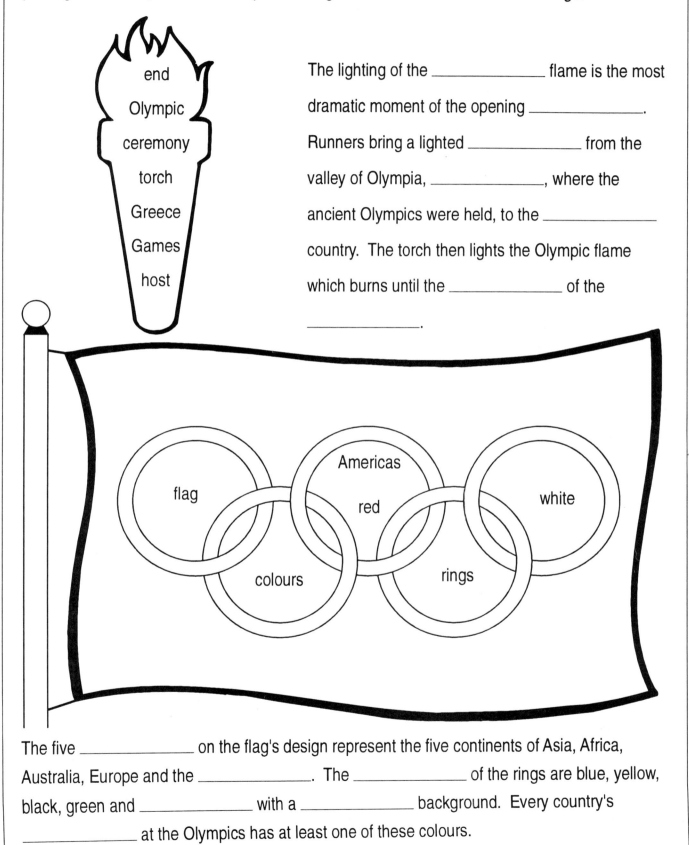

Words on torch: end, Olympic, ceremony, torch, Greece, Games, host

The lighting of the _____ flame is the most dramatic moment of the opening _____. Runners bring a lighted _____ from the valley of Olympia, _____, where the ancient Olympics were held, to the _____ country. The torch then lights the Olympic flame which burns until the _____ of the _____.

Words on rings: flag, colours, Americas, red, rings, white

The five _____ on the flag's design represent the five continents of Asia, Africa, Australia, Europe and the _____. The _____ of the rings are blue, yellow, black, green and _____ with a _____ background. Every country's _____ at the Olympics has at least one of these colours.

Colour the rings in their correct colours.

The order is BLUE, YELLOW, BLACK, GREEN, RED starting from the left.

Prim-Ed Publishing — The Olympics, Atlanta 1996

Where are the Games Held?

In 1996 the Olympic Games will be held in the city of _____, in the State of _____, in the country of the _____ _____ _____ _____.

Put the following words in their correct positions above.

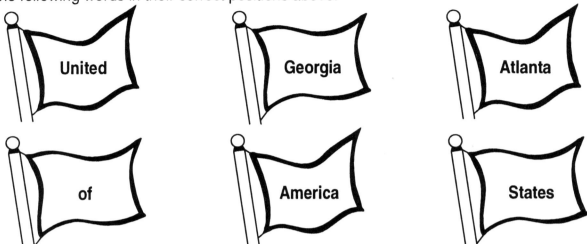

On the world map below, label the state of Georgia and colour the USA in red.

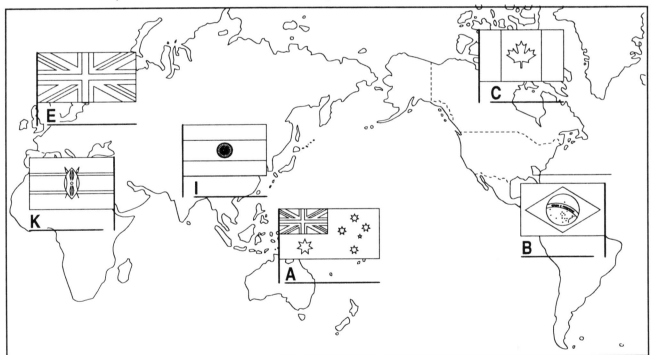

Colour the flag designs of each of the countries shown on the world map which will compete at the Atlanta Olympics.

Name each country under its flag design.

Circle the colours used on the flag designs for these countries.

    Red   Purple   Orange   White   Black

    Green   Yellow   Blue   Pink

All About Atlanta

Look at the map of the United States of America.

Colour in the state of Georgia green.

Write down the names of the five states which are neighbours to Georgia.

1. T_____
2. N_____ C_____
3. S_____ C_____
4. F_____
5. A_____

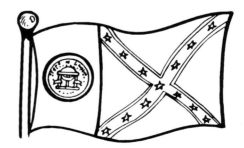

Atlanta is the capital city of Georgia. Georgia has a population of about 5.5 million. Is this

more   or   **about the same**   or   **less**   than the population of the county in which you live?

- The Olympics, Atlanta 1996 -

Medal Tally Sheet

Choose six countries, including your own, and place them on the Medal Tally Sheet. Tally the medals as they are won, and find the totals at the end of the Games.

Country	Gold	Silver	Bronze	Total
My country is…				

1. Which of these countries has the largest population? _____

2. Which is the largest country in area? _____

3. Which country received the most gold medals? _____
   _____ How many? _____

4. Which country received the most medals? _____
   _____ How many? _____

5. How many gold, silver and bronze medals did your country receive?

   Gold _____   Silver _____   Bronze _____

Opening Ceremony - Team Order

The Olympic teams march into the stadium at the opening ceremony in alphabetical order. However, the Greek team is always first, in honour of the ancient Greek Games. The host country always enters the stadium last.

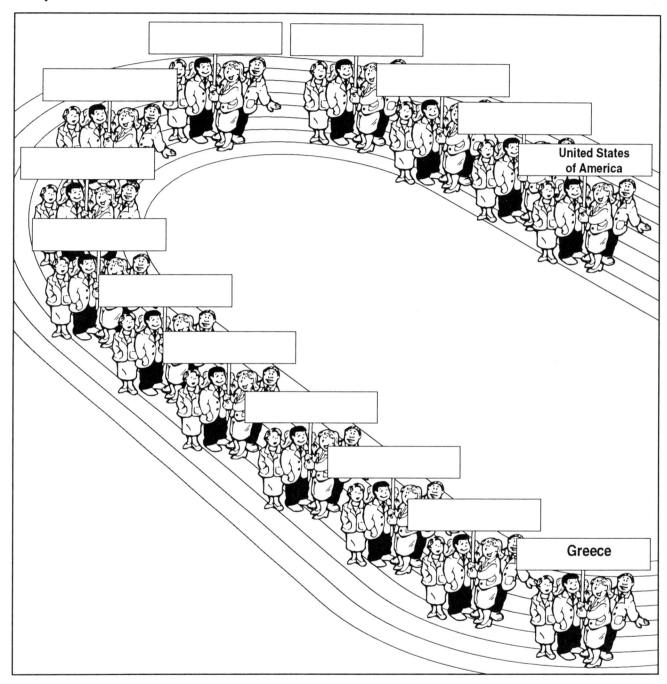

Put the following countries in their correct order as they will march into the stadium.

New Zealand	Germany	Sweden
Canada	Australia	China
Nigeria	Zimbabwe	Russia
Great Britain	Japan	Netherlands

Read and Draw

Read the following passages and draw all the details in the boxes below.

Bang! The gun went off in a puff of smoke. The Canadian girl in her red top, shot out of the blocks, followed by the New Zealand runner. The other six runners made a rainbow of colours in the lanes.

The crowd was cheering wildly as the British, Australian and American swimmers swam towards the pool wall. With one last kick, the British girl slapped the wall with a splash - and won the gold!

In which sport would you be most likely to compete? _____

Why? _____

Draw a picture of yourself winning the gold medal in that sport.

- The Olympics, Atlanta 1996 -

Equipment Maze

Follow the lines from the sport to the equipment needed to participate in that sport.

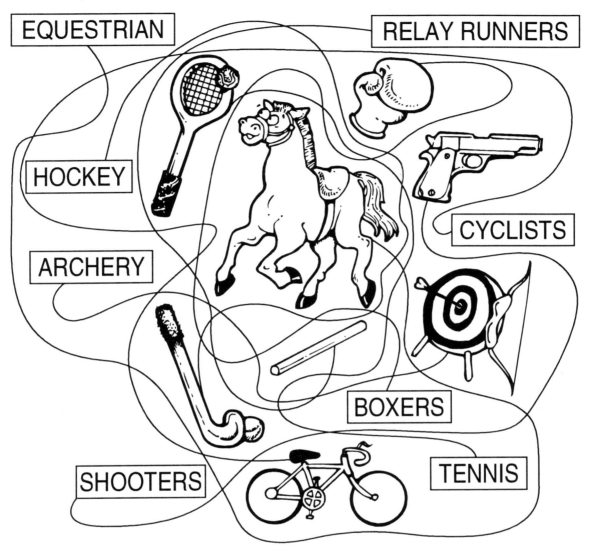

1. **Fill in the equipment needed by these sports people:**

   tennis   -   r_____   hockey   -   s_____

   equestrian   -   h_____   archery   -   b_____ and a _____

   cyclists   -   b_____   boxers   -   g_____

   relay runners - b_____   shooters -   p_____

2. **What equipment might the following athletes need?**

   divers: _____

   gymnast: _____

   weightlifter: _____

   javelin thrower: _____

Prim-Ed Publishing — The Olympics, Atlanta 1996

Measuring Athletes

❖ Measure how far the Olympic cyclists rode in their competition.

(1cm = 1km)

START

FINISH

The cyclists rode _____ km.

❖ How far were these shotputs thrown?

(a) Australia: _____
(b) Belgium: _____
(c) Canada: _____
(d) Denmark: _____
(e) Great Britain: _____

Which country won the gold medal? _____

❖ If an Olympic swimming pool is 50 metres long, how many laps are swum in:

(1) a 4 x 100-metres medley relay? _____
(2) a 1500-metre freestyle? _____
(3) a 200-metre butterfly race? _____
(4) a 800-metre freestyle? _____

What is a sprint race? _____

What is a marathon race? _____

- The Olympics, Atlanta 1996 -9-

The Olympic Motto

The Olympic Motto is written in Latin. It says:

CITIUS, ALTIUS, FORTIUS.

This means: **FASTER, HIGHER, STRONGER!**

What is a motto? _____
_____
_____

Can you think of three Olympic sports for each part of the motto in which you can go *FASTER*, HIGHER, or S<small>TRONGE</small>R? Draw a picture for each, and label the sport.

F A S T E R			

H I G H E R			

S T R O N G E R			

Which do you think would be the easiest to improve? Speed, height or strength?
_____ Why? _____

Ideals and Aspirations

The Olympic Ideal came from a sermon by the Bishop of Pennsylvania in 1908. It said:

> 'The important thing in the Olympic Games is not to win but to take part; the important thing in life is not the triumph but the struggle; the essential thing is not to have conquered but to have fought well.'

What do you think the Bishop was trying to say? _____
_____
_____
_____

Do you agree with the Olympic Ideal? Give reasons for your opinion.
_____
_____
_____

Do you think this quote only applies to the Olympic Games and sport? _____

To what other life experiences might this quote apply? _____
_____
_____
_____

Find the dictionary meanings for the following words:

triumph: _____
_____

conquer: _____
_____

essential: _____
_____

struggle: _____
_____

Olympic Winner

How would you feel if you won an Olympic gold medal?

Imagine you are standing on the dais receiving a gold medal and a bouquet of flowers. The medal is around your neck.

Some of these words might help you to write your story.

pride faster trying
effort team
exhausted record
breathless finish-line
outstanding straining excitement

- The Olympics, Atlanta 1996 -12-

Atlanta Road Map

The athletes need to go to many places when they visit Atlanta. Can you help them find where to go by using the grid map below? Don't forget to read the horizontal axis first.

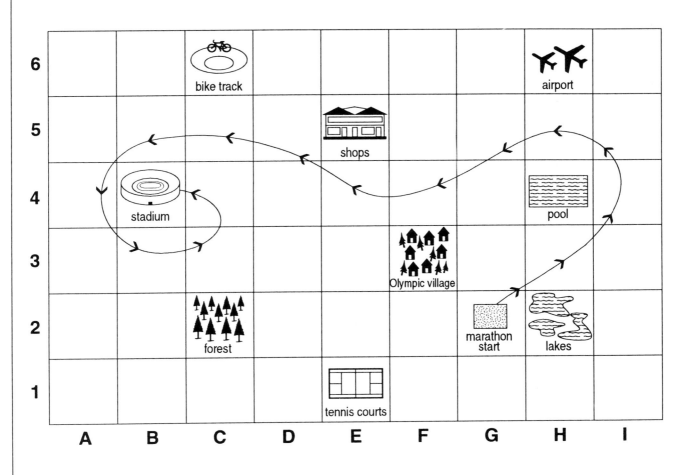

1. What can be found at (B,4)? _____
2. What is at (C,2)? _____
3. The important buildings at (F,3) are _____
4. The swimming will be raced in the pool at (____,____).
5. The marathon begins at (____,____) and ends at (____,____).
6. What event might be held at (H,2)? _____
7. To buy souvenirs you might go to (____,____).
8. The cyclists need to go to (____,____) for their event.
9. What event will be played at (E,1)? _____
10. When the games finish, athletes go to (____,____) to fly home.

❖ Add some more important places on the grid that the athletes may need to know! Colour these.

— The Olympics, Atlanta 1996 —

Sporting Word Puzzle

Use the clues given below to find the answer to an Olympic sport. The answer appears *down* the page.

1. _ _ R _ _ _ _ _
2. _ H _ _ _ _ _ _ _
3. _ J _ _ _ _ _ _
4. _ _ J _ _ _ _ _
5. _ M _ _ _ _ _ _ _
6. _ _ _ _ T _ _ _ _
7. _ P _ _ _ _ _ _ _ _
8. _ _ S _ _ _ _ _
9. _ _ _ F _ _ _ _
10. _ _ _ S _ _ _ _
11. _ _ S _ _ _ _ _
12. H _ _ _ _ _ _ _ _
13. _ _ T _ _ _ _

Clues:

1. This sport is done in a canoe, on a calm river or lake
2. A hammer is needed in this sport
3. A long, pointy spear which is thrown into the air
4. These people make decisions as to who is the winner
5. A long race usually run through the streets
6. Athletics is _____ and field events
7. Gymnasts use these to swing on
8. Runners competing in the 100 metres are known as _____
9. The last race to decide the winner
10. Where all the athletics are held
11. Sport held in a pool
12. Jumping over a small bar in a short race
13. Archers aim at a _____

Answer: The sport is _____

- The Olympics, Atlanta 1996 -14-

Prim-Ed Publishing

Good Food for Athletes

To keep their strength and energy during competition, athletes need to eat the correct foods!

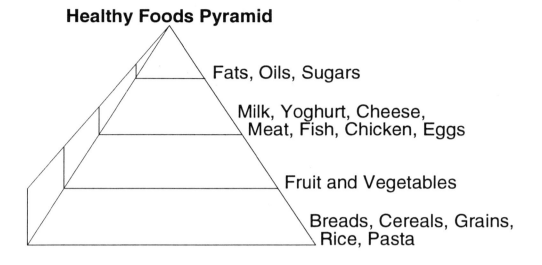

Healthy Foods Pyramid
- Fats, Oils, Sugars
- Milk, Yoghurt, Cheese, Meat, Fish, Chicken, Eggs
- Fruit and Vegetables
- Breads, Cereals, Grains, Rice, Pasta

❖ **Draw some examples of each food type on the pyramid.**

We need to eat mostly _____.

We should only eat a little of _____.

❖ **Of the foods below circle those which are important to competitors for maximum energy.**

❖ **Make up a special sandwich for an athlete's lunch.**   ❖ **Draw your sandwich below.**

Ingredients:

_____

_____

_____

_____

Mask of a Greek God

In the ancient Games, the athletes were trying to be as fast and as strong as the Greek gods. Find the names of three Greek gods.

❖ _____   ❖ _____   ❖ _____

Colour the mask of your Greek god below and cut out the eyes and mouth. Attach elastic to the holes on the sides and become a Greek god - perhaps even Zeus, the King of gods!

Sporting Shapes

Cut out the shapes below the dotted line and glue them onto the weightlifter. Label the shapes.

oval
triangle
pentagon
circle
rectangle
semi-circle
parallelogram
cube

World Records

How about making up some funny and unusual world records?

Cut out the titles on the left of the page and join them to the people on the right of the page. You can even make up some of your own!

Cut off the section at the bottom of the page to make up a class book of world records.

The World's Wildest	Mushy Squasher
The World's Smelliest	Pop Sitter
The World's Busiest	Bubble Blower
The World's Cleanest	Honey Cutter
The World's Loudest	Spot Picker
The World's Roundest	Bongo Biter
The World's Weirdest	Sneaker Sniffer
The World's Most Energetic	Dob Spotter

✂ -

My description of the world's _____

is _____

- The Olympics, Atlanta 1996 -18-

Prim-Ed Publishing

Marathon Maths

Follow the runner's footsteps around the marathon course and complete the maths problems to the finish line!

How many minutes and seconds did you take? _____ mins _____ secs.

Score _____

START

- 14 + 9
- 5 + 7
- 18 + 4
- 17 − 4
- 20 × 3
- 13 + 10
- 6 × 4
- 40 − 20
- 15 + 6
- 9 × 3
- 16 − 9
- 18 + 6
- 8 × 3
- 5 × 4
- 21 + 4
- 30 + 8 =
- 30 − 12
- 24 − 3 =
- 6 × 2 =
- 14 + 13
- 60 + 30
- 40 − 6 =
- 50 + 50
- 12 × 2
- 22 − 5
- 17 − 5 =
- 11 × 3
- 19 + 8 =
- 6 × 5 =
- 8 × 2 =

FINISH

- The Olympics, Atlanta 1996 -

Picture Codes

Can you read the letter that Shelley wrote when she was in Atlanta? Write the words under the picture codes.

D +   D's h   Mum,

_____   _____   _____,

 g   u   w+   2   h+

_____   __   _____   __   _____

about   m   tr + s   2   Atl +  +a?

_____   _____   _____   __   _____?

'm   having   nt   l    of   f .

__   _____   _____   _____   __   _____.

    1   my   h   a

__   __   __   _____   a

s g    medal.

_____   medal.

S    u   s

_____   __   _____

    + ey

_____ _____

- The Olympics, Atlanta 1996 -

Team Numbers

Some Olympic sports are played in teams. Find out how many people compete in these sports as a team.

Team Sport	Number of Competitors
4 x 100m Relay	
Hockey	
Kayak Tandem	
Basketball	
Rowing - Double Sculls	
Swimming - Freestyle Relay	
Synchronised Swimming - Duet	
Table Tennis - Doubles	

What number do the words *duet, doubles, pair, tandem* and *duo* relate to? _____

How many competitors in each of the following events?

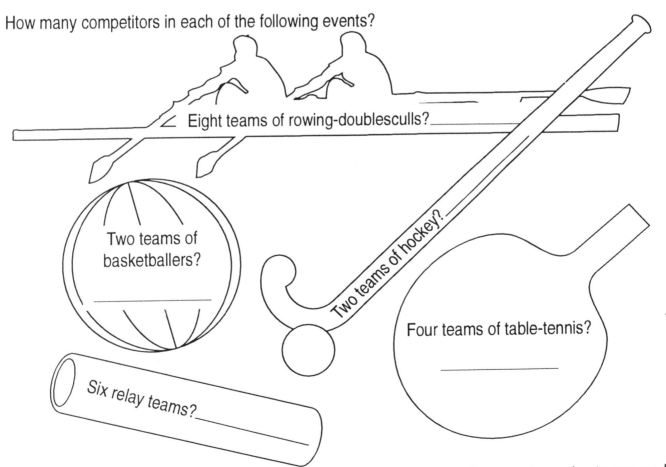

Eight teams of rowing-doublesculls? _____

Two teams of basketballers? _____

Two teams of hockey? _____

Four teams of table-tennis? _____

Six relay teams? _____

How many people on a bus carrying one hockey team, two basketball teams, two relay teams and four coaches?

Don't forget the bus driver? Answer: _____

Busy as Bees

Athletes lead a very busy life — training, practising, exercising and competing. Find all the Olympic words in the beehive word sleuth!

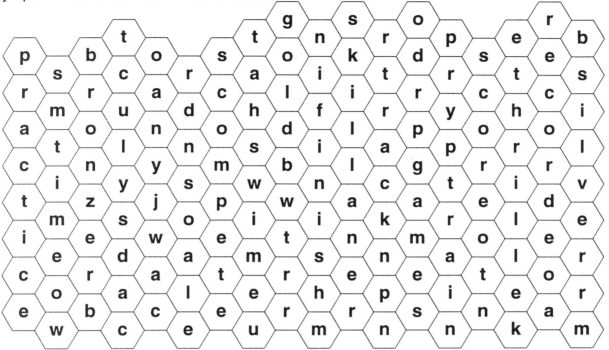

❖ Colour them as you find them.

compete	gold	win	pride	medal
score	finish	team	thrill	games
time	train	torch	flag	water
silver	bronze	track	try	skill
practice	record	swim	run	race

❖ Now put the beehive words in alphabetical order.

1. _bronze_
2. _____
3. _____
4. _____
5. _____
6. _____
7. _____
8. _____
9. _____
10. _____
11. _____
12. _____
13. _____
14. _____
15. _____
16. _____
17. _____
18. _____
19. _____
20. _____
21. _____
22. _____
23. _____
24. _____
25. _win_

Fit and Healthy Body - 1

Cut and paste the parts of the skeleton onto the correct place in the body outline on the next page.

Write the common name for each body part next to its scientific name. You may use your dictionary to find the answers.

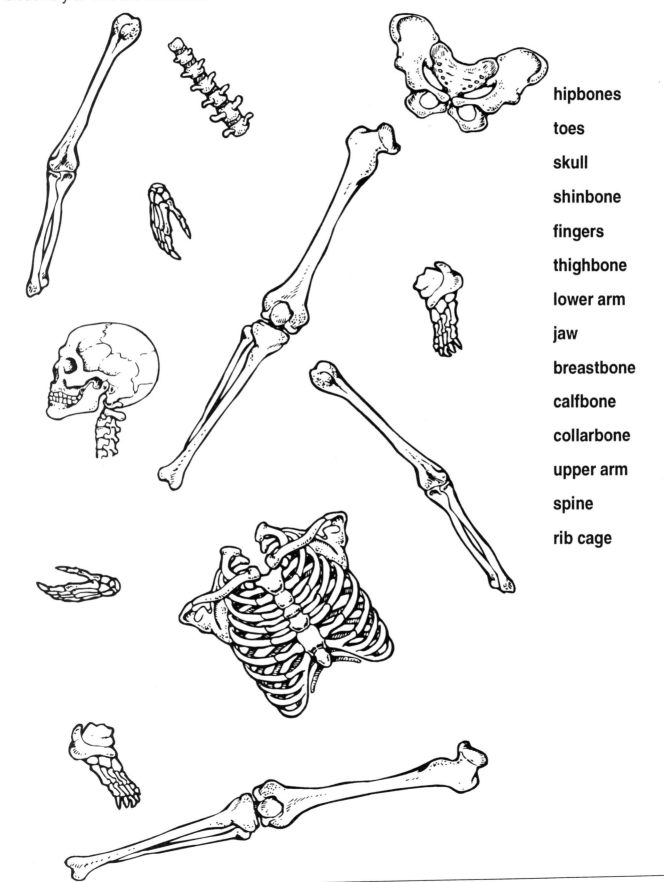

hipbones

toes

skull

shinbone

fingers

thighbone

lower arm

jaw

breastbone

calfbone

collarbone

upper arm

spine

rib cage

Fit and Healthy Body - 2

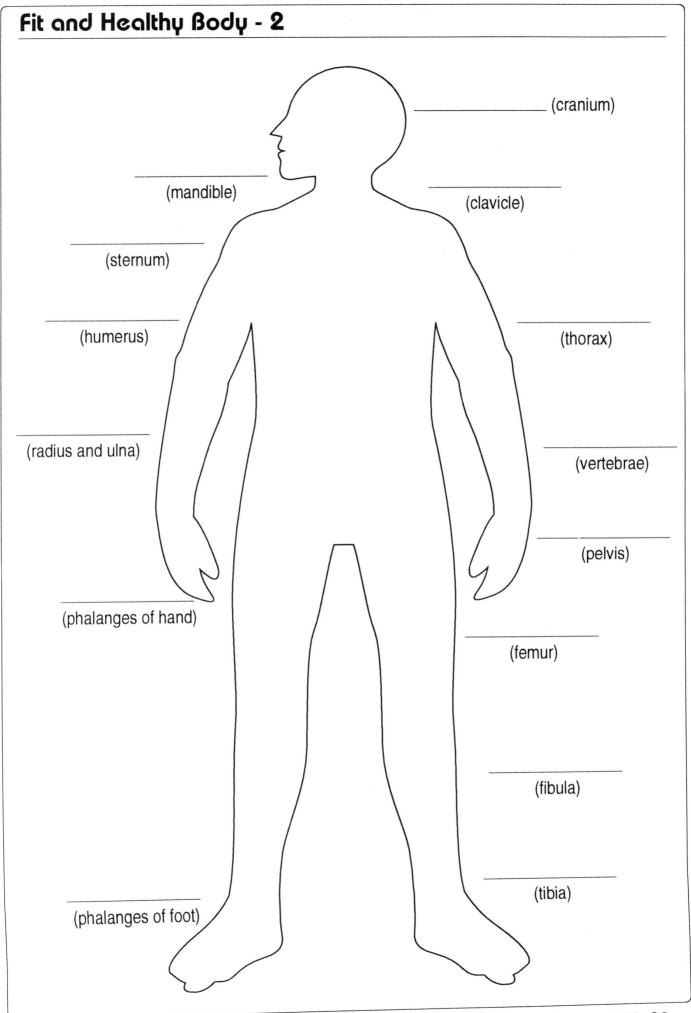

Coins of the USA

The following coins are currently used in the United States of America. These American coins will be used by the Olympic athletes from all over the world to buy items they may need during their stay in Georgia.

1. Two inscriptions are written on the 'head' side of the coin, apart from the year the coin was minted. They are:

    (a) _____

    (b) _____

2. What two main pieces of information are written on the 'tail' side of each coin?

    (a) _____

    (b) _____

3. What coins would you need to buy these items:

    (a) 4 shoelaces at 20 ¢ each?

    _____

    (b) 1 tube of toothpaste at 95¢?

    _____

    (c) 3 oranges at 25¢ each?

    _____

    (d) Phone call home at $4.30?

    _____

    (e) Writing paper and envelopes at $2.15?

    _____

Design a special one dollar coin to commemorate the 1996 Atlanta Olympics.

- The Olympics, Atlanta 1996 -

Special People

To compete in the Olympic Games means that a person is one of the very best athletes in the world. This means they are very special people.

❖ Put a circle around 12 of the words below which you think might describe an Olympic athlete. Add three more of your words describing a special Olympic athlete.

tired strong hardworking lonely talented busy silly intelligent musical

perfect calm special powerful sleepy ordinary hungry active dedicated

positive lazy athletic friendly beautiful nervous fast anxious

Write the 15 words you have chosen onto the Olympic medal below, and colour the medal in gold, silver or bronze.

Cut out your special people medal and hang them around your classroom.

- The Olympics, Atlanta 1996 -

Team or Individual Sports?

Complete the sentence below:

Some events at the Olympic Games are team games, which means _____

_____

_____

Others are individual events, which means _____

_____

_____

Sort out the events below into team or individual events and write them in their correct boxes.

Team Events

Individual Events

- The Olympics, Atlanta 1996 -27-

Prim-Ed Publishing

Disabled Sports

Competitive sports are not only restricted to the able-bodied sportspersons. Disabled sportspeople compete internationally in the Paralympics. This is the equivalent to the Olympic Games. There are over 20 sports involved!

Find out about these physical disabilities.

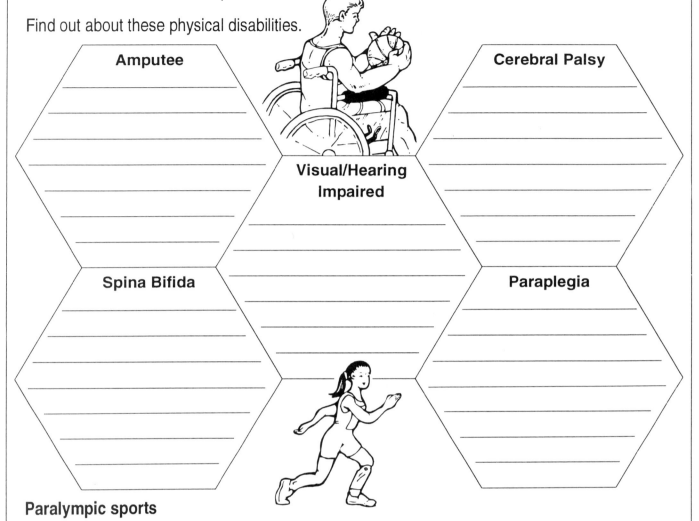

- Amputee
- Cerebral Palsy
- Visual/Hearing Impaired
- Spina Bifida
- Paraplegia

Paralympic sports

yachting   shooting   athletics   cycling   archery   lawn bowls   swimming   basketball
racquet ball   judo   boccia   powerlifting   table tennis   fencing   volleyball   tennis
football   equestrian   goal ball

1. Underline those sports which could be played in a wheelchair.
2. Circle those sports which could be played by an amputee.
3. Put an asterisk next to the sports which could be played by a visual or hearing impaired sports person.
❖ Discuss and write down some facilities that need to be provided in the stadium and the games accommodation for wheelchair athletes.

_____

❖ Why is the Paralympics an important sporting event?

Relaxing is Important

Although the athletes have to train very hard to keep fit, they also need to relax after their training so their bodies do not become too tired.

Athletes might relax by _____

or _____

_____

❖ List four ways you like to relax:

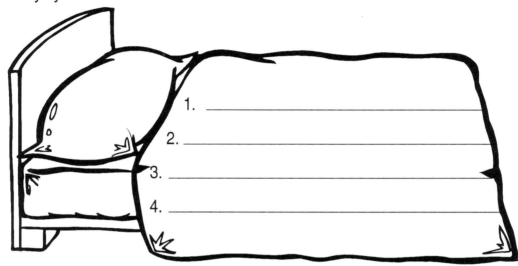

1. _____
2. _____
3. _____
4. _____

❖ Circle the time segment and colour in the clock times which show the times you relax the most!

8.00 a.m.   -   12.00 (noon)

12.00 (noon) -   3.00 p.m.

3.00 p.m.   -   6.00 p.m.

6.00 p.m.   -   8.00 p.m.

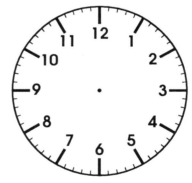

❖ Put a circle around the activities below which are relaxing - (no stress!).

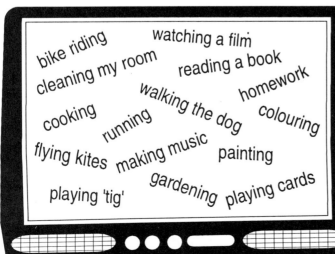

bike riding, watching a film, cleaning my room, reading a book, cooking, walking the dog, homework, running, colouring, flying kites, making music, painting, playing 'tig', gardening, playing cards

❖ The best way I like to relax is:

_____

_____

with _____

_____

_____

- The Olympics, Atlanta 1996 -

Sports Words Jumble

Jumbled Words

Can you unjumble these Olympic sports?

1. nioBxg _ _ _ _ _ _ _
2. geFnicn _ _ _ _ _ _ _
3. seTnin _ _ _ _ _ _
4. vnDiig _ _ _ _ _ _
5. cykHoe _ _ _ _ _ _
6. doJu _ _ _ _
7. chAryer _ _ _ _ _ _ _
8. wiRogn _ _ _ _ _ _
9. ccSeor _ _ _ _ _ _
10. ginCcyl _ _ _ _ _ _ _

Circle Sentence!

Begin at the arrow. This is the first letter of the sentence. Miss every second letter as you read around the circle. Stop at the full stop!

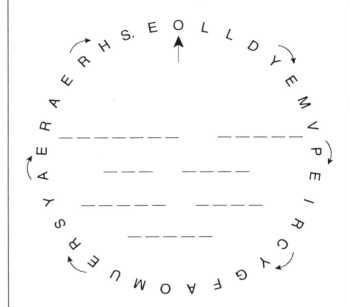

Write out your sentence on the lines in the middle of the circle.

Wonder Words:

How many new words can you make using the letters in the word below?

TABLE TENNIS

_____
_____
_____
_____

Missing letters:

Add the vowels a, e, i, o or u to make these Olympic sports.

1. J__v__l__n
2. Gymn__st__cs
3. S__cc__r
4. W__ __ghtl__ft__ng
5. Sh__ __t__ng
6. B__sk__tb__ll
7. W__t__r P__l__
8. M__r__th__n
9. Sw__mm__ng
10. __thl__t__cs

Magic Words:

Write the opposite of these words. A word will appear in the box going down.

Rough	_ _ _ _ _
Pull	_ _ _
In	_ _ _
Polite	_ _ _ _
Bottom	_ _ _

Racquet Jumble

How many table tennis racquets can you count? _____ Colour each a different colour.

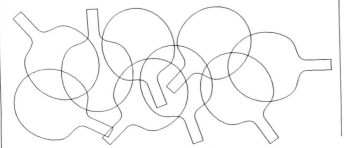

- The Olympics, Atlanta 1996 -

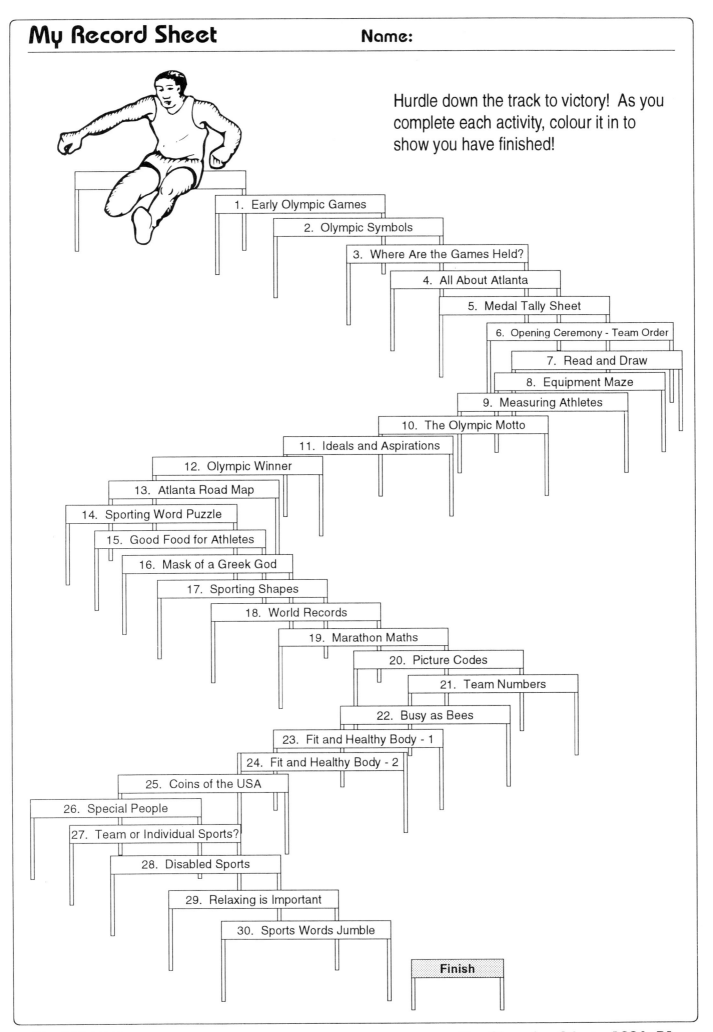

Quiz Questions

Read the following set of questions to the class. Children write their answers in groups or individually. Answers to each question are given in brackets.

1. Is the sport of fencing a summer or winter sport? (summer)
2. On what part of the body is the skull? (head)
3. What was the prize for winning an event in the ancient Olympic Games? (wild olive wreath)
4. What is the name of the long distance road race at the Olympic Games? (marathon)
5. True or false? Breads and cereals are good foods for athletes. (true)
6. Name the capital city of Georgia. (Atlanta)
7. How many circles do the Olympic Rings have? (five)
8. What is the colour of the winner's medal of an Olympic event? (gold)
9. Who was the King of the gods in Ancient Greece? (Zeus)
10. Which country enters the Olympic Stadium first at the opening ceremony? (Greece)
11. In which country is the state of Georgia? (USA)
12. How many runners are in a relay team? (4)
13. Is gymnastics a wet or dry sport? (dry)
14. How many cents is a quarter worth? (25¢)
15. True or false? Diving is a team sport. (false)
16. What is the Olympic motto? (faster, higher, stronger/citius, altius, fortius)
17. How often are the Olympic Games held? (every four years)
18. What is lit at Olympia and carried to the host city? (Olympic torch)
19. How many competitors in a kayak tandem event? (two)
20. True or false? The host country enters the stadium last at the opening ceremony. (true)
21. What are the colours of the medals for the second and third place-getters for an Olympic event? (second-silver, third-bronze)
22. What does an equestrian need to compete in his or her Olympic event? (horse)
23. What is the part of the skeleton which protects your heart and lungs? (rib cage)
24. What are the five colours of the Olympic rings? (blue, yellow, black, green, red)

Answer Sheet - Middle primary

Page 1: 1. an olive wreath 2. 776 BC 3. false 4. (a) to worship the gods (b) to show their strengths 5. peace and friendship 6. luxury 7. every 4 years 8. true 9. festival

Page 2: (a) Olympic, ceremony, torch, Greece, host, end, Games. (b) rings, Americas, colours, red, white, flag

Page 3: Atlanta, Georgia, United States of America.
Great Britain, Kenya, India, Australia, Canada, Brazil

Page 4: 1. Tennessee 2. North Carolina 3. South Carolina 4. Florida 5. Alabama

Page 6: Greece, Australia, Canada, China, Germany, Great Britain, Japan, Netherlands, New Zealand, Nigeria, Russia, Sweden, Zimbabwe, United States of America

Page 8: 1. tennis-racquet, equestrian-horse, cyclists-bicycle, relay runners-baton, hockey-stick, archery-bow and arrow, boxers-gloves, shooters-pistol
2. divers-pool, gymnast-parallel bars, balance beam, pommel horse, weightlifters-weights, javelin thrower-javelin

Page 9: The cyclist rode 37.5 km.
Shotputs - Australia 5m, Belgium 6m, Canada 3.5m, Denmark 7.5m, England 5m. Denmark won the gold medal.
Swimming - 1. 8 laps, 2. 30 laps, 3. 4 laps, 4. 16 laps
Sprint - short distance Marathon - long distance

Page 10: A motto is a short saying expressing the ideals of an organisation.

Page 13: 1. Stadium 2. forest 3. Olympic village 4. (H,4) 5. (G,2) and (B,4) 6. Rowing 7. (E,5) 8. (C,6) 9. Tennis 10. (H,6)

Page 14: 1. rowing 2. hammer throw 3. javelin 4. judges 5. marathon 6. track 7. parallel bars 8. sprinters 9. final 10. stadium 11. swimming 12. hurdling 13. target The sport is weightlifting.

Page 15: We need to eat mostly breads, cereals, fruit and vegetables.
We should only eat a little of fats, oils and sugars.

Page 19: 23, 12, 22, 13, 60, 23, 24, 20, 21, 27, 24, 7, 25, 20, 12, 24, 21, 38, 18, 27, 24, 90, 17, 34, 12, 100, 33, 30, 27, 16.

Page 20: Dear Dad and Mum, Do you want to hear about my trip to Atlanta? I'm having a lot of fun. I won my race and a gold medal. See you soon, love Shelley.

Page 21: Team sports: 4 x 100 relay - 4, Hockey - 11, Kayak Tandem - 2, Basketball - 5, Rowing - 2, Swimming relay - 4, Synchronised swimming - 2, table tennis - 2.
Duet, doubles, pair, tandem + duo relate to 2.
Rowing double sculls-8x2 = 16. Basketball-2x5 = 10. Hockey-2x11 = 22. Table tennis-4x2 = 8. Relay-6x4 = 24. People on the bus - 34.

Page 22: Alphabetical order: bronze, compete, finish, flag, games, gold, medal, practice, pride, race, record, run, score, silver, skill, swim, team, thrill, time, torch, track, train, try, water, win.

Page 24: Cranium-skull, clavicle-collarbone, thorax-ribcage, vertebrae-spine, pelvis-hipbones, femur-thighbone, fibular-calfbone, tibia-shinbone, phalanges of foot-toes, phalanges of hand-fingers, ulna and radius-lower arm, humerus-upper arm, sternum-breastbone, mandible-jaw.

Page 25: 1. (a) In God We Trust (b) Liberty
2. (a) The country in which the coins are minted - USA. (b) The value of the coin.
3. Answers will vary

Page 27 Team games are events where more than one competitor represents a country.
Individual events are where only one competitor represents a country in that event.
Individual Events - wrestling, diving, boxing, long jump, judo, hammer throw.
Team events - basketball, water polo, soccer, relay-running, volleyball.

Page 28: Amputee - an arm or leg amputated, spina bifida - meninges of spinal cord protruding through a gap in the backbone, causing paralysis, visual/hearing impaired - blind or deaf, cerebral palsy - impairment of muscle function and weakness of the limbs, paraplegia - paralysis of the lower part of the body.
Wheelchair: shooting, archery, basketball, athletics
Amputee: shooting, athletics, archery, lawn bowls
Visual/hearing impaired: shooting, athletics, cycling, archery, lawn bowls, swimming, basketball, judo, boccia, powerlifting, tabletennis, fencing, volleyball, tennis, football, equestrian, goalball.
Facilities needed: wheelchair ramps and disabled toilet facilities.

Page 30: Jumbled words: boxing, fencing, tennis, diving, hockey, judo, archery, rowing, soccer, cycling.
Circle sentence: Olympic Games are held every four years.
Racquet jumble: there are nine racquets.
Missing letters: 1. Javelin, 2. Gymnastics, 3. Soccer, 4. Weightlifting, 5. Shooting, 6. Basketball, 7. Water polo, 8. Marathon, 9. Swimming, 10. Athletics.
Magic word: SPORT

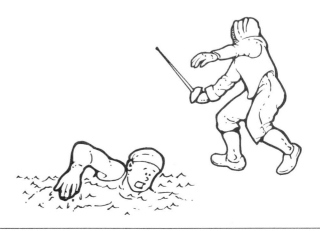